Stand Up to Bullying
Growing Character

By Frank Murphy

Published in the United States of America by
Cherry Lake Publishing
Ann Arbor, Michigan
www.cherrylakepublishing.com

Reading Adviser: Marla Conn, MS, Ed., Literacy specialist, Read-Ability, Inc.

Photo Credits: ©Veja/Shutterstock, cover, 1; ©Rido/Shutterstock, 4; ©Monkey Business Images/Shutterstock, 6; ©Rawpixel.com/Shutterstock, 8; ©Cheryl Casey/Shutterstock, 10; ©Oksana Shufrych/Shutterstock, 12; ©Sussi Hj/Shutterstock, 14; ©Golden Pixels LLC/Shutterstock, 16; ©Monkey Business Images/Shutterstock, 18; ©LightField Studios/Shutterstock, 20

Copyright © 2020 by Cherry Lake Publishing
All rights reserved. No part of this book may be reproduced or utilized in any form or by any means without written permission from the publisher.

Library of Congress Cataloging-in-Publication Data

Names: Murphy, Frank, 1966- author.
Title: Stand up to bullying / written by Frank Murphy.
Description: Ann Arbor : Cherry Lake Publishing, [2019] | Series: Growing character | Audience: K to Grade 3. | Includes bibliographical references and index.
Identifiers: LCCN 2019007446 | ISBN 9781534147393 (hardcover) | ISBN 9781534148826 (pdf) | ISBN 9781534150256 (pbk.) | ISBN 9781534151680 (hosted ebook)
Subjects: LCSH: Bullying—Juvenile literature. | Bullying—Prevention—Juvenile literature.
Classification: LCC BF637.B85 M874 2019 | DDC 302.34/3—dc23
LC record available at https://lccn.loc.gov/2019007446

Cherry Lake Publishing would like to acknowledge the work of The Partnership for 21st Century Skills. Please visit *www.p21.org* for more information.

Printed in the United States of America
Corporate Graphics

CONTENTS

5 What Is Bullying?

9 How Bullies Hurt People

17 Ways to Stop Bullying

22 Glossary

23 Find Out More

24 Index

24 About the Author

Bullies can make kids feel unhappy and uncomfortable.

What Is Bullying?

Bullying happens when one person or a group of people pick on someone. Bullying is a mean **behavior**. It's how some people make fun of someone. It might also frighten that person. Bullying is not something that happens just once. It happens over and over again.

Some bullies make people feel bad by saying mean things about them.

Bullies pick on people in different ways. Some say bad things about them. Others might trip someone, and then point and laugh at that person. Some bullies make people feel like they are not a part of a group.

Think!

Have you ever been bullied? How did it make you feel? Were you scared? Have you ever acted like a bully yourself? Think about how your actions can hurt others.

Bullies might make fun of other kids for the clothes they wear or the way they look.

8

How Bullies Hurt People

Sometimes bullies pick on people who are different from them. A bully might make mean **comments** about the way a person looks. The comment might be about someone's clothes or glasses. It could be about someone's **culture** or background, like a country they are from or a religion they follow.

Some bullies threaten to harm kids to scare them.

A bully is usually trying to **embarrass** someone. It often makes a bully feel more powerful than the other person. Most times, the bully already has some form of power over the person they are bullying. The bully might be older or bigger or stronger. Sometimes the power comes from a group picking on one person.

Being bullied can make kids feel like they don't fit in at school.

Some bullies might say, "You don't belong here," or "Don't sit at our lunch table." These are examples of ways that bullies make others feel bad or unwanted. People who are bullied often end up feeling like they aren't good enough. But this is wrong. All people should feel included and should be treated with **respect**.

Watch!

Watch the kids on your playground. Are they friendly? Do some of them act like bullies? See how bullies try to make other kids feel bad. How can you act to make sure you're not a bully?

Bullies often corner their victims in places where adults can't see them.

Bullying can happen almost anywhere. It might happen on a playground at recess. It could be in a neighborhood at a park. It could happen at school in places where adults are watching many kids and don't notice the bullying. Bullies usually choose places and **situations** where adults can't see them being mean.

Ignoring bullies is one way to try to deal with them.

Ways to Stop Bullying

If you are ever bullied, you will probably feel bad because of it. You may feel like yelling or crying. These feelings are normal. One thing you can try to do is to walk away or **ignore** the bully. Some people pretend that the bullying doesn't bother them. A bully who doesn't get a **reaction** might leave that person alone.

Inviting someone to sit with you at lunch is a great way to help that person feel included.

If you see a person being bullied, you can try to help. Invite the person being bullied to sit at your table. Offer to work with the person on a class project. You and your friends might tell the bully to leave the person alone. Sometimes a bully will change their actions when a larger group stands up to them.

Create!

Write a play about bullying. Include characters who are bullies and characters who are victims. Have your friends play those roles—and then switch. See how different being the bully feels from being the victim.

Talking with an adult can help you deal with bullies.

You may need to talk to an adult about what is happening. Adults don't always know there is a problem until you tell them. By telling an adult you trust, you are showing that you are smart and strong in asking for help. An adult can help you find ways to deal with the bully and can find ways to make the bad behavior stop.

GLOSSARY

behavior (bih-HAYV-yuhr) the way someone acts

comments (KAH-ments) words that explain your thoughts about something

culture (KUHL-chur) the ideas, customs, and traditions of a group of people

embarrass (em-BAR-uhs) make someone feel awkward or uncomfortable

ignore (ig-NOR) to pay no attention to something or someone

reaction (ree-AK-shuhn) an action in response to something

respect (rih-SPEKT) a sense of caring for someone else's worth

situations (sich-oo-AY-shuhnz) the conditions that exist at a certain time and place

FIND OUT MORE

BOOKS

Ferry, Beth. *Stick and Stone*. New York, NY: Houghton Mifflin Harcourt Books for Young Readers, 2015.

Hall, Pamela. *A Bully-Free Playground*. Minneapolis, MN: Magic Wagon, 2013.

Hall, Pamela. *A Bully-Free School*. Minneapolis, MN: Magic Wagon, 2013.

Ludwig, Trudy. *The Invisible Boy*. New York, NY: Knopf Books for Young Readers, 2013.

Sornson, Robert, and Maria Dismondy. *The Juice Box Bully: Empowering Kids to Stand Up for Others*. Northville, MI: Ferne Press, 2010.

WEBSITES

KidsHealth—Dealing with Bullies
http://kidshealth.org/kid/feeling/emotion/bullies.html
Find out about bullies and how to handle them.

Stop Bullying
www.stopbullying.gov
Learn about bullying and how to prevent it.

INDEX

adults, 14, 15, 20, 21
asking for help, 20, 21

bullying
   how it hurts people, 9–16
   how to stop it, 16–21
   what it is, 4–8
   where it happens, 15

clothes, 8, 9
cornering someone, 14
culture, 9

differences, 9

embarrassment, 11

fitting in, 12

ignoring bullying, 16, 17
including someone, 18, 19

laughing at someone, 7
lunch, 18, 19

making fun, 5, 8

picking on someone, 5, 7, 11

power, 11

religion, 9
respect, 13

saying mean things, 6, 7, 9, 13
scaring people, 5, 10
school, 12, 13, 15, 18, 19

threats, 10

ABOUT THE AUTHOR

Frank Murphy has written several books for young readers. They are about famous people, historical events, and leadership. He was born in California but now lives in Pennsylvania with his family. Frank thinks the best way to stop bullying is for everyone who sees bullying to stop being a bystander!